A Fraction's Goal—
Parts of a Whole

To Noreen,
who cuts my burdens in $\frac{1}{2}$

—B.P.C.

Fraction:
A part of a
whole number

A Fraction's Goal—Parts of a Whole

by Brian P. Cleary

illustrated by Brian Gable

M Millbrook Press / Minneapolis

Fractions are a portion,

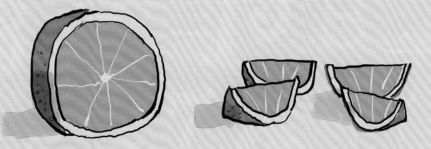

a piece,

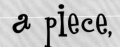

or just a part

of something that is larger,
like this segment on this chart.

Or look at this round pizza.
It can be cut in 2

or 4

or 6

or 8 or more—
whatever best suits you.

But let's say that it's cut in 2
and you pick up 1 slice.

If you've got 1 piece out of 2, it's $\frac{1}{2}$ to be precise.

So now, if someone wants $\frac{1}{2}$, 2 slices will be needed.

$\frac{2}{4}$ and $\frac{1}{2}$ are the same;
they're different ways to read it.

Fractions also work with groups, like $\frac{2}{3}$ of the players,

$\frac{7}{8}$ of jugglers,

and $\frac{1}{2}$ of the mayors.

Pretend you have 3 uncles and 2 came for a visit.

That would mean $\frac{2}{3}$ were there.
That's not so hard now, is it?

Let's say the third one then showed up
to join in all the fun.

That's 1 whole group of uncles,
'cause $\frac{3}{3}$ equals 1.

Fractions come in handy if you ever help with baking.

You'll see them in the recipes

for breads and cakes you're making.

$\frac{3}{4}$ tablespoon of salt . . .

add $\frac{2}{3}$ cup of flour . . .

22

$\frac{5}{8}$ cup of chocolate chips . . . .

and bake for $\frac{1}{2}$ hour.

The numerator is the word for the number that's on top.

Like the 3 that's in, "We lost $\frac{3}{10}$ of this year's crop."

The number underneath the slash
is a denominator.

Note that nearly all the time
this bottom number's greater.

You'll know more than just a portion
if you give them half a chance!

So, what is a fraction?
Do you know?

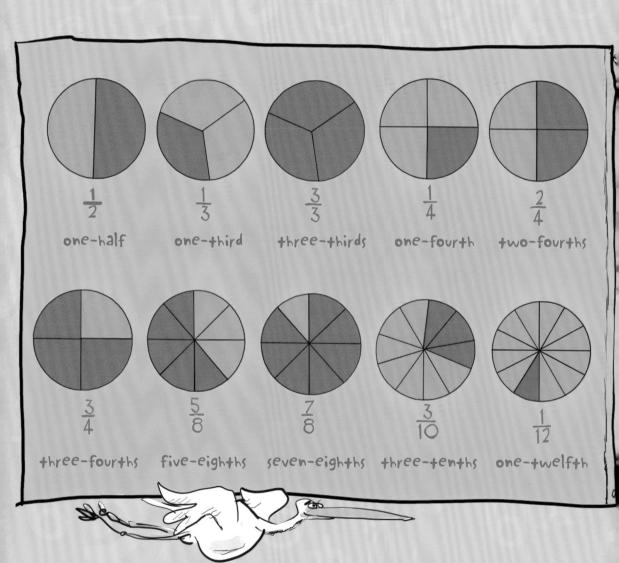

$\dfrac{1}{2}$ one-half

$\dfrac{1}{3}$ one-third

$\dfrac{3}{3}$ three-thirds

$\dfrac{1}{4}$ one-fourth

$\dfrac{2}{4}$ two-fourths

$\dfrac{3}{4}$ three-fourths

$\dfrac{5}{8}$ five-eighths

$\dfrac{7}{8}$ seven-eighths

$\dfrac{3}{10}$ three-tenths

$\dfrac{1}{12}$ one-twelfth

ABOUT THE AUTHOR & ILLUSTRATOR

Find activities, games, and more at www.brianpcleary.com

BRIAN P. CLEARY is the author of the best-selling Words Are Categorical© series as well as the Math Is Categorical©, Food Is CATegorical™, Adventures in Memory™, and Sounds Like Reading© series. He has also written Six Sheep Sip Thick Shakes: And Other Tricky Tongue Twisters, The Punctuation Station, and several other books. Mr. Cleary lives in Cleveland, Ohio.

BRIAN GABLE is the illustrator of many Words Are Categorical© books and the Math Is Categorical© series. Mr. Gable also works as a political cartoonist for the Globe and Mail newspaper in Toronto, Canada.

Millbrook Press
A division of Lerner Publishing Group, Inc.
241 First Avenue North
Minneapolis, MN 55401 USA

For reading levels and more information, look up this title at www.lernerbooks.com.

Main body text set in RandumTEMP 35/48.
Typeface provided by House Industries.

Library of Congress Cataloging-in-Publication Data

Cleary, Brian P., 1959–
    A fraction's goal : parts of a whole / by Brian P. Cleary ; illustrated by Brian Gable.
        p.   cm. — (Math is CATegorical)
    ISBN: 978-0-8225-7881-9 (lib. bdg. : alk. paper)
    ISBN: 978-0-7613-8045-0 (EB pdf)
    1. Fractions—Juvenile literature. 2. Ratio and proportion—Juvenile literature. I. Gable, Brian, 1949- ill. II. Title.
QA117.C54 2011
513.2'6—dc22   2010051518

OCT 2 4 2016

Manufactured in the United States of America
5-41518-8699-3/17/2016